DEPRESSION BUT LOVE

A Christ-Centered Guidebook to
Overcoming Depression through the Love of God.

Tiffani:
    God knows your heart
    and He knows somethins
    here will bless you.
        [signature]

DEPRESSION BUT LOVE

A Christ-Centered Guidebook to
Overcoming Depression through the Love of God.

DANIELA LARCO PAIR

XULON PRESS ELITE

Xulon Press
2301 Lucien Way #415
Maitland, FL 32751
407.339.4217
www.xulonpress.com

Paperback ISBN-13: 978-1-6628-0978-1
Ebook ISBN-13: 978-1-6628-0979-8

In memory of my dear friend
Tracy

National Suicide Prevention Lifeline
1-800-273-8255

But as for you, you thought evil against me; but God meant it unto good, to bring to pass, as it is this day, to save many people alive (Gen. 50:20).

TABLE OF CONTENTS

INTRODUCTION

When depression claimed the lives of three of my friends, I decided to research and write about it. I hope that my perspective, as well as the testimonies of other people fighting this disease, will provide a better understanding about how this emotion attacks and what we can do to be set free from it. This is a guide and a way to help the fight against emotional oppression. This book describes depression and how to overcome it. There are many sources of depression, but what I have found is that relationships are a leading cause.

The start date for this book was delayed, because I waited until I felt ready to face the multiple challenges I knew would come with writing about depression and other mental illnesses. The time had to be right, and I was aware that with every powerful weapon I used, opposition might come. I was not ready to deal with possible conflicts and emotional distress the enemy could bring.

When my friend, Tracy, took her life, I went to a very dark place. It was the morning of April 16, 2015. I was driving home from a doctor's appointment, at which the doctor told me how concerned he was for my health. I was reflecting on my time on earth and was in deep prayer about my life. I was asking the Lord to grant me wellness and to allow me to stay in this dimension a little longer, so I could raise my kids and serve His purpose. I was on Facebook looking at my newsfeed and read a very hurtful post. My dear friend, Tracy, had passed away. There was no information on how she passed. I was told days later that she had taken her life. When I found out that my friend did not pray to God to better her life but instead took it upon herself to end it, I was in shock. I found myself filled with questions and anger, which allowed the enemy to infiltrate my mind. I immediately started to experience anxiety attacks, nightmares, and insomnia.

Doctors are quick to give pharmaceuticals for emotional distress and mental disorders. Without being asked too many questions, I was given narcotics to help me deal with Tracy's death and to stop the emotional pain, and the medicine made me feel like a zombie. It helped for a moment. But after fourteen hours of being out of it and not present with my kids, I decided to seek the Lord in the midst of the crazy storm. I called on the name of Jesus with all my heart, and there He appeared. He showed up as He has always done before. My Father, the great Healer and Physician, took care of me, providing peace and comfort in spite of unanswered questions.

> *Do not be anxious about anything, but in every situation, by prayer and petition, with thanksgiving, present your request to God. And the peace of God, which tranced all understanding, will guard your hearts and your minds in Christ Jesus* (Phil. 4:6–7).

As I sat at my friend's funeral, I wondered about life and death, and about depression and love. When Tracy was being placed in the ground, I realized I would never see my friend again. Not here again on earth or in this body. Would I see her in heaven? Why did she not call me? Why did she not care about her daughter or her family? I had so many questions to ask, but at that point it felt like none of them really mattered anymore.

The day was nice, and the sun was shining. I was standing by a tree with tears streaming down my face when, all of a sudden, a peaceful wind stirred up. As the wind touched my face and hair, it also felt as if it touched my spirit. It was at that very moment the Lord gave me this revelation: If we stop rationalizing everything, we will find out that there is always beauty and purpose in madness and sorrow.

This book is in memory of my beautiful friend Tracy. I hope to be a voice for love and for those who are suffering from multiple attacks, like depression, anxiety, bipolar disorder, etc. It's important to realize that in this world of fast solutions and quick-fix pills, there is another answer for our brokenness.

"Nothing is new under the sun." Eccles. 1:9. This book is a compilation of what is already out there. It's glued together with the many stories contained within this book that I have heard after years of street ministry, stories that have been shared with me through interviews and the divine inspiration of the Holy Spirit. I am grateful for all the amazing people who have shared their thoughts, feelings, and emotions on the subject of depression, those who opened their hearts and let me see inside to their deepest distresses. I am thankful for all the obedient people who have written books, filmed videos, or preached sermons about mental health issues. Because you have decided to read this book, whether for yourself or a friend, I believe that God's will for you is in the pages to come.

I have faith that you will use this book as a weapon to help recognize attacks of the enemy. His ultimate plan is to turn us against ourselves, fill us with guilt, and separate us from the Lord. Not everything is an act of evil. As humans, we have been given the ability to discern and control our own thoughts. Gaining control over our minds will result in the freedom to walk fully in purpose, serving efficiently and in favor of the kingdom of love. A kingdom with a King who knows only how to love and be loved. A kingdom that was brought to us with Emmanuel. God walking with us, among us, and to defend us, where unity, mutual affection, abundance, wellness, and more are given to us for our enjoyment.

> *We are pressed on every side by troubles, but we are not crushed. We are perplexed, but not driven to despair. We are hunted down, but never abandoned by God. We get knocked down, but we are not destroyed. Through suffering, our bodies continue to share in the death of Jesus so that the life of Jesus may also be seen in our bodies* (2 Cor. 4:8–18).

DEPRESSION IS THE ABSENCE OF LOVE

D arkness is nothing but the absence of light, just as cold is the absence of heat.

It makes sense then to think that as darkness is the absence of light and cold is the absence of heat, depression is the absence of love.

Love. What a big and magical word. Four simple letters, yet it's so complex. Many of us struggle to understand love. The reality is right in front of our eyes, and it's more tangible than what we may believe. If we seek love, we will be able to recognize it, receive it, and finally be greatly empowered by it.

I have spent a lot of time surveying people to help determine their experience with this wonderful feeling of love. Do you think there is one person in the world who hasn't experienced love? To come across the smallest acts of kindness, a warm smile or a word of encouragement, can make us feel valued and acknowledged. This feeling may last only seconds or for years, but the point is all humans have experienced some type of love at least once in their lifetimes.

If we are able to feel love, even when surrounded with chaos and negative emotions, then it seems love is constantly floating in the atmosphere and always available around us.

Depression, also known as major depressive disorder, is a mood disorder that makes you feel constant sadness or lack of interest in life. Most people feel sad or depressed at times. It's a normal reaction to loss or life's challenges. But, when intense sadness—including feeling helpless, hopeless, and worthless—lasts for a week or more and keeps you from living your life, it may be something more than sadness. (WebMD, 2020)

It sounds very heavy. But it's definitively not a virus or a bad gene. It seems to me that depression has a lot to do with negativity that comes from within. Depression is, for the most part, a twisted emotion, passed on through broken people.

Throughout the years, I have talked to hundreds of people about their emotions. After listening to their stories, I've concluded that depression is a mechanism compounded by multiple factors that, when taken all together, are toxic for our minds, bodies, and spirits.

Neuroscience is defined by Merriam Webster as "deals with the anatomy, physiology, biochemistry, or molecular biology of nerves and nervous tissue and especially with their relation to behavior and learning." To me, I understand neuroscience is the in-depth study of our internal hard drive and how it can affect our entire lives. The subconscious is the place that records every moment we experience in life, even the details that we are not aware of when we are totally present.

Our conscious mind is the present moment and can be at war with the subconscious. The subconscious can bring memories into our conscious mind that were buried in the past and that can affect our present reality. Most of the time, our actions and feelings are a response of the subconscious. Therefore, we sometimes remember the most random things without even thinking about them, like a song, a place, or a smell, et cetera.

The human mind is amazing, but it is also very fragile. If we experience something that is reckless to our emotions, it will not just be recorded but will impregnate our innermost being.

3

A good friend of mine and a great woman of God told me she had experienced depression and even contemplated suicide. Judging from who I know her to be, I would have never thought she dealt with suicidal thoughts. To me she seems so joyful and solid in her understanding about love and God. While married to her first husband, she experienced physical and mental abuse. She was young and had dreamed of being happily married, as many young girls do. She expected her marriage to last her whole life. She was not expecting the dream to become a nightmare. He often attacked her verbally about the way she looked, critiquing her weight and calling her names. This happened day after day after day.

If someone close to us repeatedly puts us down or continually spews negative remarks, eventually we will believe them. We will start to manifest what has been spoken to us, and the negativity becomes our reality.

Words are so powerful. As the scripture says, *Life and death are in the power of the tongue* (Prov. 18:21). I love science, because it studies God's way of moving, creating, and transforming. Quantum physics has proven that words indeed have a vibrational effect that moves in our atmosphere, by either creating or destroying.

Confusion, fear, hurt, and disappointment were engraved in my friend's mind. This was all it took to make her feel worthless and forget her real value. She forgot how to appreciate herself and the way she is loved by God.

Like a subliminal message, these words were played over and over in her mind, magnifying all of the other bad emotions and becoming so overwhelming she considered putting an end to the hurt. This man exhibited a loveless behavior toward her. He did not show respect, kindness, patient, tolerance, or anything resembling unconditional love. His ability to express love was damaging to her, and it turned into depression in my friend's life. I asked my friend what prevented her from killing herself and how she managed to stop listening to the negative voices in her head. She told me it was through people at her church. They started noticing how she had withdrawn, and reached out to her, showing her love. She had a choice—she could continue to tap into that negative part of her being or choose to receive all the beauty of unity and love. Thankfully, she chose the most powerful weapon. Her fear was gone, the negative voices were cast out, and her ability to love herself started to come back.

Our minds, bodies, and souls are perfectly aligned, and all need each other. A distressed soul will bring a stressed mind and therefore a sick body. I believe that chemical imbalances, as science calls it, can be the result of those three elements being out of balance. I don't want to underestimate the benefits of medicine for some. But medicine should not be the only approach. Medicine should be used as a stepping-stone, as we work on changing patterns in our thinking process. We need to make a conscious decision to allow God's presence to heal us with His loving power.

My friend's ex-husband abused her, even though he thought he loved her. How can we argue with an abuser, who swears to love the victim? His need to be acknowledged was deeper than a simple desire; it was most likely a desperate call for attention. Sadly, the way he manifested that need for attention became a horrible reality. This guy claimed to follow the Lord; he was a believer! Why would a person claiming to be on the side of love not share the love of God with others? An atheist coworker of mine, in one of our many conversations about God, told me that God is nothing but an emotion that people create to feel better. Little did he know that I agree with him. For us to experience the spirit of freedom and feel more than an emotion, only in our mind, we are to seek understanding of His supernatural and unconditional adoration for us. The divine spirit of God will never impose Himself to us. He only comes inside when we welcome Him in. The transformation starts to happen when and if we are willing to let go of destructive patterns and unnecessary beliefs. The knowledge in our minds is not enough, if we cannot open our hearts and lessen our pride.

Our society has confused feeling of fulfillment with true love. The meaning of affection is so twisted from what it's truly intended to be that it confuses the minds of some people. Often times, we view love as attraction, chemistry or good sex. Many are engaging in relationships that rely solely on false imaginations that, at the end, wound the heart. We have been influenced by romantic movies, and now social media, to believe that love is about physical or financial standards.

> *Hope deferred makes the heart sick, but a*
> *longing fulfilled is a tree of life* (Prov. 13:12).

LOVE IS THE BEST MEDICINE

The cure for depression is to have an abundance of what it lacks—the agape love of God! I have seen in my life and in the lives of others that without a deep relationship with our Creator, we are left to swim alone in an ocean of broken souls. We are walking in darkness, striving to find the light. If we think of ourselves only as empty shells and not as God's creation, then we are ignorant and have what I call low spiritual self-esteem. Changing our views about our existence, to understand that we are souls traveling inside a body, can be life changing. When we live more aware of our eternal reality, little things that seemed important will no longer bother us. Seeking the power of God within is not just a never-ending adventure, it also brings healing, transformation, and purpose! As we travel in this world, in search of God's blessings and with a clear vision, everything will start to fall in place. We will start opening realms of abundance we used to only dream about.

> *But seek first the Kingdom of God and His*
> *righteousness, and all these things will be*
> *given to you as well* (Matt. 6:33).

Why does a supernatural, loving, and holy God love us humans? This is a question that has crossed my mind after watching the news and witnessing all the bad things that we, as a species, are capable of doing. And, it's not only the terrible, immoral, and illegal things we do, it's also how we take care of ourselves in ways that go against what is healthy and good for our well-being.

The answer is simple and evident. But it seems to be rejected by some. He created us in His image and likeness and for us to enjoy and rule over all creation. The benefits to us, as Children of God, are immeasurable. God did not create us without a master plan. He intended for us to rule and have dominion over everything on earth!

God has great adoration for us. His heart is full of passion toward His children because we are a reminder of His very own nature. He desires to have a personal relationship with us, to guide us on how to gain fellowship with Him, and to move us into His kingdom forever. He is so fond of us that He broke the barrier of space and time in choosing humanity, leaving a peaceful, joyful, and perfect world to walk among us in an imperfect, painful, and dark place. He, in the form of His Son, Jesus, came to teach us how to make things possible, if we believe. We need to stop being carnal and see beyond our sinful nature. He gave us the key to eternal life, giving us victory over the major curse we brought to ourselves—death!

Jesus came to model the life we are supposed to be living and enjoying abundantly, regardless of the negativity that is all around us. The power that rests in the life and death of Jesus is the bridge to our freedom.

Very truly I tell you, whoever believes in me will do the works I have been doing, and they will do even greater things than these, because I am going to the Father (John 14:12). Wow, this is a breakthrough against the depression of these days! We can choose to receive forgiveness for all our misconduct and selfish ambitions. We can forgive those who hurt us and damaged our minds, hearts, and spirits through their misbehavior. We can choose to love others as we love ourselves. We can choose to speak life or death, blessings or curses.

We can create our reality to be more beautiful, because we can rebuke what is evil, negative, and dark, and we can manifest only what is good, pure, and genuine.

> *Truly I tell you, whatever you bind on earth*
> *will be bound in heaven, and whatever*
> *you lose on earth will be loosed in heaven*
> (Matt. 18:18).

Think about all the amazing things we can accomplish, both as individuals and collectively. Think of the incredible advancements in technology and science alone. There are so many genius minds bringing greatness. How about when people come together to rebuild someone's house or give food and aid to disaster areas? The marvelous miracle of life inside a woman's womb is incredible. We are a fascinating creation, seemingly taken out of a fantasy or science fiction book. The crazy thing is, we are real, our dimension is real, life is real, and manifesting what God has for us is real. It's all just one positive thought away, just one right intention away.

People with depression may not be capable of seeing themselves in the light of this truth. It is sometimes easier to blame God or be angry with Him. It takes away our responsibility for overcoming the negative and stepping into His kingdom's power. The good news is the Lord is fighting our battles! He promised He will never leave us and never forsake us. He gave us the gift of eternal life and redemption. His deepest desire is for us to find our identity. We can be free from oppressive lies and negative patterns, and we can start to walk in

11

the freedom of His love and our true destiny. Reaching the sovereignty of God is not easy, if we try to do it alone. We sometimes need someone to motivate us and something to believe in. Finding someone to love is not the answer to our long-term loneliness, taking a drug will not take the pain away indefinitely, and having money will not bring us a life of happiness.

The first step to our restoration is accepting that our fellowship with our Heavenly Father has been broken. In the same manner that children need of their parents to be functional and emotionally stable, we need Aba Father to enjoy of a sound mind.

From that realization, recognizing, understanding, and receiving Jesus as the bridge is the next step to freedom. His sacrifice paid the debt for our transgressions (things we do against the holy nature of our creation). He walked the road of darkness, feeling rejected, abandoned, and betrayed, yet He did not quit His mission. Some of His life's purpose was to save us from eternal loneliness and to teach us how to love others. His death gave us victory over sin, and His resurrection left us with power over death. His mission was to die in the most humiliating and horrible way, so that we can use Him as our advocate and obtain all God's favor in this life and the next one. After we believe in Jesus as our Savior, we are responsible to take the steps needed to grow in the spirit. Cultivating a relationship with the Holy Spirit, which is the Spirit of God and Jesus living inside us, is not different from any other relationship in our lives. Quality time and the desire to know about this divine trinity are essential to becoming friends with this amazing power that resides inside and all around us. Loving ourselves and allowing His wisdom to reveal to us what steps we must take to obtain the abundant life that Jesus promised us is the goal. When we achieve that, we will be ready to love others with the same self-lessness and passion.

Jesus is the Son of God, the greatest teacher ever known. If Jesus' popularity was ranked for the total number of followers in our social media, He would be known as the greatest influencer of all time. Jesus is the master of speaking life. He granted us the ability to use our words to create our reality. His life impacted history, dividing the eras and creating a movement that is ever growing.

Jesus is the real meaning of unconditional love manifested in human form.

In the movie, *The Passion of Christ*, we can see Jesus struggling with a spirit that is pressing down on His soul with fear, anxiety, panic, sorrow, sadness, loneliness, and other tormenting emotions. Jesus cried out to our Father, and God gave Him the strength to carry onward to the cross, so that He could save us all. I can imagine all hell breaking loose at that very moment to stop our Savior from His mission. His humanity is what gives us access to an abundant life. Jesus kept himself sober-minded (a clear focus on the truth of God), through all the agony. He was able to take control of His emotions, and God gave Him the power to overcome the condemning demons. Jesus was so collected during all the prophesies being fulfilled, even knowing all the horrors awaiting Him. Jesus worked in conjunction with the Holy Spirit to disintegrate fear and conquer death. *There is no fear in love. But perfect love drives out fear because fear has to do with punishment. The one who fears is not made perfect in love.* (1 John 4:18).

It is in Him, and through Him, that we can tap into supernatural strength, while overcoming the negative emotions that are ruling our lives and derailing us from reaching our true purpose. If Jesus had let Satan oppress Him with fearful emotions that day at Gethsemane, there would have been a different outcome for humankind, an outcome I do not want to think about.

We get to help ourselves and believe in the goodness of God. I believe in the famous Greek expression: "God helps those who help themselves." I have experienced this in my own life. I know the only way to freedom is to break the chains that keep us tied to sin and broken-ness. The Lord is the energy behind the supernatural strength that we need to make this happen.

> *Not by power not by might but by my Spirit*
> *declares the Lord of hosts* (Zech. 4:6).

His spirit is love, and love is the ultimate and most powerful source of life. Because, God is love, creation is love, eternal life through the cross is love, and abun-dance and walking in purpose is also love.

Depression can present feelings of neglect and rejec-tion.And the depressed person can express those same negative feelings to another person.We pass on these horrible feelings from one human to another, creating patterns that go on for years or decades, and from gen-eration to generation.The underlying feeling pushing these negative emotions and manifesting in our reality is often fear.The belief that we are not worthy of love and the lack of hope that we will find love creates a big emptiness in the heart. It can lead to anxiety, panic attacks, bipolarity, and many other mental disorders. With this emotion out of control the pressure becomes too difficult to be processed all alone. Some of us may try to alleviate the feeling of solitude in our souls or fill the emptiness in our hearts by taking actions that are not guided by love but are instead detrimental to our destiny. Making unwise or bad choices when we feel confused or fearful usually causes feelings of guilt and shame. When living a guilt-driven life, rather than a thriving one, a sorrowful spirit will experience gloomy and dark days. And, in some cases, this will lead to a desire to end the misery.

Being ready to make a commitment to ourselves is essential for change. Openness and clarity are keys to gaining awareness of the tools that are within us for victory. Jesus promises an abundant life for those who believe and can plug into the realm of love. I will provide some tips and exercises in the "Tips to Help Beat Depression" section that have helped me stay connected with God. I have been able to understand Jesus' command to love God with all our hearts, souls and minds, as well as loving myself by keeping my cup overflowing, so I can give the best of me in loving others. This is the perfect combination for a joyful life and kingdom advancement.

It has been a long journey from the moment I started to write this book. Part of it has been the responsibilities of this life, the interview process, and dealing with emotional matters myself. I experienced a big pull to find that forever partner, making that a priority over my purpose. In that search, I lost heart and was thrown into the wilderness. I was lost spiritually as well. I was able to live the Bible verse that explains what takes place in the mind when the heart is broken. How, suddenly our thoughts go into the rabbit hole, making us lose all reason about ourselves and the plans God has for us. God's extraordinary existence is so real. And so is Jesus and the plan of salvation. Restoration through the cross and the promise of new life through resurrection is like oxygen, it's the breath in our lungs. By His divine presence and the power of unconditional love, I was awakened to the Holy Spirit and brought out of that terrible time. I will share my experience in more detail as part of the "Relate" section of this book.

There is no fear in love; perfect love drives out all fear. So then, love has not been made perfect in anyone who is afraid, because fear has to do with punishment. There is no fear in love; instead, perfect love drives out fear, because fear involves punishment (1 John 4:18). I don't believe hate is the opposite of love, even if it seems logical that it would be. The opposite of love is fear, because fear causes us to doubt ourselves. It questions our existence, it whispers negative ideas to us, it gives us reasons to question the fact that we have been given power to overcome the shadows that cloud our spiritual radar. Fear is one of the main emotions that stops us from reaching our full potential in all areas of our lives—mentally, emotionally, spiritually, physically, and financially. I have chosen fear so many times, even something as simple as the fear of flying, fear of the dark, fear of quitting a bad relationship, or fear of pursuing my dreams. I missed out on freedom, joy, authenticity, and identity because of extreme worries and apprehension.

> *For God did not give us the spirit of cowardice but of power and love and self-control* (2 Tim. 1:7).

We were built with strength, goodwill, and a sound mind. This is certain for those who see themselves through Jesus' eyes and His full potential.

Fear is not always bad. Fear is part of our human nature; it keeps us grounded to the fact that we depend on love more than anything. When we feel intimidated or under pressure, it is instinctive to react and take action. It is instinctive for us to protect ourselves from pain, much like running from an aggressive dog to avoid being bitten. We are quick to react in the face of fear. And, with any fear we should be ready to move to action. If we get paralyzed, we aren't able to think clearly, and that allows the fog to fall on us. Blurry vision will prevent us from moving forward with joy and hope for the future. Trusting our intuition and giving into God is moving fast. Staying stuck or drowning in hurt emotions allows this feeling to control our lives. It robs us of the promises that God has for those with a vision, His vision! If we are afraid of being alone, the action we should take is to join a church,　　a bowling team, a hiking group, or anything where we can create community and healthy bonds. Most people with depression will instead stay home and seclude themselves for fear of rejection. If we are afraid of not being able to pay the bills, the action should be to get an additional job, a different job, trade careers, or find some other form of income. However, some of us let the fear of not having enough time to enjoy life, or not being good enough, get in the way of our success. When we allow fear to become panic, it can make us run in the opposite direction of our true destiny. We could be buying into the lie that will ultimately blind us from our own true self and derail us from our God-given purpose.

Nothing in this world is darker than spiritual darkness. Nothing can give us more scarcity than the lack of vision. Nothing is more depressing than living a life as orphans not knowing our identity, separated from others and without a purpose. We should continuously seek for revelation of our origin. We should always strive to have a relationship with our Father, and we should embrace, with confidence, the fact that everything has been given to us as children of the highest.

How can we identify fear from being a normal emotion or an oppressed emotion that is opening doors to torturing spirits or negative energies? I believe the manifestation is evident. Being held back from true happiness, peace, and abundance is not from the Lord of freedom. At this point, self-reflection is a must. We need to understand why we have a lack of trust in God and get to the root of the distrust. His Word helps us to know God's character. Reading the Bible is the best way to understand who God is and find teachings on how to live right. He says we are His, and we were indeed created in His image. His Word says we are fearfully and wonderfully made. His Word says we are redeemed from the curse of death into eternal life. It is through Jesus that God empathized with us, and that is how we can identify with Him as well. He was the Son of God walking on earth to witness for us our true abilities and our authority. Before ascending, Jesus told the disciples He must leave so that the Holy Spirit can dwell in us. This will give us a way to have supernatural encounters with the Father and to all kinds of heavenly realms. Jesus said that we will be able to do the same things He did and even more. That means we can speak things in faith, and we will see them manifest in a tangible way in our reality. There is an abundance the positive and uplifting statements His Word declares about us; indeed, there are more positive affirmations on our behalf than negatives curses.

POSITIVE VERSUS NEGATIVE FEELINGS

Depression, for many, is like companionship. It becomes the very thing that defines a person's character, robbing them of their identity. We tend to own negative feelings, because we are familiar with them and they make us feel comfortable, even when they are destructive. What I find amazing is how unaware we are that we can choose the feelings we want to live with. The negativity, Satan, the dark side, whatever you prefer to call it, can only impact our emotions as much as we allow. But a great joy for me is knowing that even as we have been given this ability, we are not supposed to do it alone. If we spend time meditating with the Lord, it can improve our moods, especially when distress is present. If done in the morning, this simple practice can change the whole outcome of our day. One thing I have come to realize is that even when we have immeasurable mental abilities to create real- ities, without faith nothing happens. I chose to put my faith in Jesus, because He is all powerful. He is my best friend and forever companion. It is through Him that I gain the confidence to push harder anytime I withdraw into fear. Remembering His unconditional love for us is humbling; it makes me vulnerable and open to receive, from Him, greater strength and affirmation.

There is a choice to make every morning, every hour, and every second. From the most basic things, like what we are going to eat, to what we are going to wear. We always get to choose. Some of these choices are vain, yet they can have an impact on the way our day goes. There are other more serious choices that, once we have made them, will affect our lives for good—things like what we do for a living, who we share our lives with, and where we spend eternity. These may be the most important decisions we will face. For me, walking with Jesus was the best choice I have ever made! I started to see myself not just as a mere human, but as an incredible creation with great capabilities to operate in supernatural love. I started to see myself as an eternal being who has a deep connection with a mighty God. It made me understand the power of sacrificial love, while not letting the love for myself disappear. Jesus' invitation to make Him the Lord of my life revealed to me the lie I was living with, the lie that I thought I could do everything on my own. It threw me into an exciting self-seeking journey of purpose, identity, and service to others. This journey is available for all who want to take it. I know for sure that walking this path with Him is a cure for depression.

FATAL LOVE

O ne of the most common triggers of depressio I n that can take people to the point of suicide is a romantic relationship.

We can call it a coincidence, but all three of my friends who took their lives had one thing in common—they were all triggered to end their lives after a failed love relationship. They were let down through either betrayal, abuse, or a toxic relationship.

I'm not saying that every person who takes their life does so because of a romantic crisis. It could be triggered by horrible memories from a strong emotional trauma like is PTSD, extreme bullying, or many other reasons.

When we find a person to love and that person gives us affection we've been craving, all of a sudden, our sense of worthiness increases. If we had been neglected, we finally feel as if someone cares and we won't be lonely anymore. An amazing fact about the process of falling in love is that our brain experiences an actual chemical reaction that leaves us exposed and open. The release of dopamine, vasopressin, adrenaline, and oxytocin at the beginning of a romantic interaction blurs our ability to reason, because it's like the feeling of being high. It makes us feel pleasure and a euphoric sense of purpose. The high is so addicting and fascinating that it can stop us from making smart decisions when deciding on a partner. But this high does not last for long. Once we are comfortable enough to expose our true selves, the pain of past wounds and fears may start to show up. Over time, as the newness and excitement settle, we might be trapped in a toxic relationship that can lead us to a deeper sorrow.

For those who deal with depression, experiencing separation from a person due to betrayal, abuse, neglect, or a broken covenant can be devastating. God intentionally gave us a deep want to be with someone, because we were made to be together as couples. When God created Adam's companion, it was not because he asked for a wife. Adam was enjoying life and fellowship with God. But God knew Adam's heart. God saw Adam and thought it was not good for him to be alone. The Lord created the beautiful process that happens when we find someone to bond with, procreate with, and enjoy the company of in a partnership. God's plan is a process to bring us purpose and fulfillment. After man's fall, through disobedience, vanity, and pride, all of God's plans and best intentions for our lives were twisted by the enemy.

When our spirit has been crushed, it's only natural that we feel the need to be whole again. Those of us who have been shattered by life events seek out wholeness. But oftentimes, when we find a partner, we become dependent of that person's moods and wants, because our partner is more than someone to share our life with. That person is more like a patch for our wounds or someone to escape loneliness with.

When that happens, our sense of value and acceptance is subject to how our partner views us and treats us. We find our sense of belonging in our partner, rather than in God and ourselves. Our partner becomes like a drug that is finally giving us the feeling our soul was craving. It's impossible, even in a healthy and mature relationship, to be happy all the time. There will always be challenging days and disagreements. But if we make our partner the center of our universe, when the euphoric feelings in the early part of the relationship stop, our old feelings of neglect, rejection, betrayal, and abandonment surface again.

The human heart was created to live in love with everything and everyone, and especially with God. For those who don't know their identity, love loses its true meaning. Lots of us dealt with effects of crushed love in our childhood, whether from our parents or other family members, or our peers. But if brokenness is all that we know, we will more than likely choose what we are used to. We will end up in similar relationships, with the same familiar feelings, hurting ourselves over and over without knowing what healthy love feels like. We often walk the same road several times, like the Israelites, who circled the hill country along the route to the Red Sea, in Deut. 2:1.

Repeating patterns are more common than we think, because we are creatures of habit. We create routines for everything we do from the moment we wake up until the moment we go to bed. We also have tendencies to get into similar situations and attract the same types of people. It's like placing the same bandage on an old wound, over and over, until the bandage does not stick anymore. Most often, we live blind to the fact that we find ourselves in the same situation again and again, with a new person. After analyzing my life and the lives of many I have talked with, I've learned that people handle breaking off toxic patterns in two ways. Some people seek help by talking with others and being proactive. They take part in things like therapy, counseling, prayer groups, spiritual awareness, and community support. Others have a hard time breaking off toxic patterns and lose strength during the fight. They fall into great despair and often lose control over their thoughts, sometimes seeing suicide as the only way out. But those who let their minds reach such despair and end their pain also begin a whole new pain for the ones they leave behind.

People struggling with depression often have a hard time separating from their loved ones, because they've become codependent on their partner. Their relationship is a patch for their wounds. We manifest how we feel, and we act out what we believe of ourselves. When all we feel is negativity, our attitude will also be dysfunctional and not appealing. People with depression usually project low self-esteem and weakness, and may be described as drowning in self-pity.

We have all experienced a broken heart. The words alone say it all—*broken heart*. When something breaks, its pieces often separate. We give pieces of ourselves to the people we deeply love in the hope of becoming whole again. We also want to get some of their essence and make it ours, so we can become one. In a healthy romantic relationship, that is the right approach, because we should give all of ourselves to our partners. But to be able to give all of ourselves, we need to learn how to be ourselves first. If we don't know who we are, and we don't know what we want, then we have nothing to offer. This situation often attracts people who also have nothing to offer. When this natural process of selection to find a partner fails, the hurt is so deep that you can physically feel it in your body. Many people describe it as an oppressive feeling in the chest and it includes other reactions, such as lack of appetite or inability to sleep. It can lower our immune system, opening the door to all kinds of negative symptoms. I remember the terrible feelings I experienced, while going through the mess of my failed marriage. It sometimes hurt so much, that my stomach would get upset. I had sweaty hands and heart palpitations. Some nights, I wasn't able to sleep. so, I overate, and gained weight and my cholesterol levels increased. I have a good friend who was also in a horrible abusive relationship. While going through her storm, she had the worst eczema I have ever seen. Her feet were so dry that they cracked open, giving her more than just emotional pain.

For people who are not haunted by depression, the heavy sadness and physical symptoms will only continue for a period of time until they find a healthy way to bounce back to their normal selves. However, for the ones who are battling depression, a broken heart could be the biggest trigger of all, taking their drained souls down a rabbit hole they can't come back from.

And, once they can't take the heaviness anymore, they decide to finish their pain in a very fast and dramatic way.

When we have our hopes rooted in the wrong things, we won't be able to stay on our feet, if the conditions are shaky. Everything will start to crumble around us, and it will bring us down, crushing our dreams and desires.

Love between two people can indeed be one of the most beautiful feelings, but it can also be destructive. The problem is not the falling in love part or the giving our all. The problem is when we place our sense of belonging in another mortal human being. We hope that person will fulfill something in our emotions that is missing, a void of some kind. We expect to feel accepted, valued, and loved. There is nothing wrong with wanting to experience those emotions; we were made to feel them all. The problem is when we don't have a clear understanding of who we truly are and who we belong to. We belong to the creator of the universe.

When I recount the suffering that I experienced when I went through a breakup, it was a sorrowful feeling of betrayal, abuse, and disappointment. There were times I would cry so loud and shed so many tears, it felt as if my soul was drowning in an ocean of hopelessness. There are many stories, poems, and songs that express the sentiment of what this pain is like. Sometimes the people who write those words turn to suicide as a way to end their misery.

The Ecuadorian poet, Dolores Veitimilla de Galindo, put an end to her life after finding out her husband was with another woman.

A verse at the end of one of her poems, translated to English, reads: "I had a delirious love for you. No, my haughtiness does not suffer your betrayal. And if I am not able to forget the traitor, I will pull my heart out of my chest!"

This verse is not figurative. Dolores really meant what she wrote. She was not able to handle the agony that this disloyalty brought to her soul.

Suicide is sometimes the only goal for those who are haunted by the shadows of depression. When trying to overcome depression, it is important to drive away our thoughts of how bad our situation is. Negative thinking gets us down into a low frequency that opens the door to spiritual forces assigned to oppress us and keep us slaves of our own obstructive emotions. I witnessed the physical pain my cousin went through due to chronic arthritis he had since he was five years old. As he got older, the physical pain worsened, due to severe degenerative joint damage. Each conversation I had with him turned into a very pessimistic experience. All he talked about was pain management and the different doctors, medicines, and treatments he was trying. He seemed to be losing track of all the goals he once had, as well as his relationship with God and the relationships with people around him. After his best friend committed suicide, the search to find a solution for his physical pain got even worse. And he almost lost his mind during his exploration. He started looking for solutions in the wrong places, because his pain, at this point, became not just physical but emotional as well. He had a big hurt in his soul. He was exposed to a near-death experience shortly after he went into his wilderness. While he was in a coma, he had a lot of people praying for him and loving on him, until the love of God reached his heart. When he recovered, he was more positive and joyful. Even though he was still hurting, he stopped concentrating only on the pain. He put time into following the Lord, loving his family, and finding purpose in his life. He was finding ways to overcome his affliction and not letting it rule his life. He found new hope in love. One year after renewing his relationship with God and his family, due to complications with his medicine, our Lord called my cousin home, while he was asleep in his bed. I am forever thankful to witness how God's grace gave this amazing guy the opportunity to find Jesus again. He left us peacefully, and now he's enjoying the promise of eternal life, free of sorrow and pain. Getting self-absorbed in our tragedies will only bring us to darkness, isolation, and sin, leading to a path of self-destruction.

> *For our struggle is not against flesh and blood, but against the rulers, against the authorities, against the spiritual forces of evil in the heavenly realms* (Eph. 6:12).

I consider myself a confident person, but when I was trying to find someone to share my life with, I started to lose the real me. I was placing my hopes in false expectations and imaginings that I created to help me feel whole. I was investing a lot of time learning how to become the best helper for a man. I was dedicated to fitting a pattern more religious than realistic, and in this process, I was losing self-love. I totally believe that we must love selflessly; however, we have to love God first, so that we can love ourselves and then others. We should have our cup so full of God's love that we can walk through life without distorted beliefs but instead be excited and strong in faith, waiting for what God has in store for us.

Receiving the unconditional love from our Heavenly Father revealed to us through His Son, Jesus, should be the main goal of our lives. Making sure we know

Jesus, and that He knows us, is the best way to become good stewards of love. If we freely receive, we should freely give.

The culture we live in conditions us to believe that we will be made whole when we find our "soul mate" or "other half." We go from person to person, not finding another part of us but instead losing many pieces of ourselves along the way.

Jesus said: *Seek the Kingdom of God first and His righteousness and everything will be added to you* (Matt. 6:33). The kingdom of God was brought to us when Emmanuel (God with us) walked the earth. He left the Holy Spirit to live inside us. The kingdom of God sits within us through the power of His divine presence that dwells at the very core of our souls. When we fall in love with God and his amazing ways, we will fall in love with ourselves. We will be able to understand the incredible passion He has for us and allow the revelation of His love to flow through us, for the benefit of others. If we could only comprehend the power that is in our inner being, along with everything that we are capable of and why God loves us. If we could only stop living in shame and guilt for the mistakes and sins we commit, if we could only accept that we are no longer confined to darkness but have been brought to light, then the shadows would no longer claim our joy and no fear would creep into our souls.

Religion has conditioned us to be guilt driven, yet a relationship with our Father is about grace. It is about open communication with God, a relationship that will lead us to a life that honors Him and others. It will lead us to the path of our true destiny. His forgiveness will wash away our guilt and shame and allow us to experience a peace that transcends understanding. If we could really grasp our actions, affecting not just us but our reality, and everyone around us, we would make more conscious decisions to be more empathetic and positive. We would be more concerned about how to help our neighbors rather than being self-absorbed in our own difficulties. We are made to live in community. We are one race—we are God's children. When one member hurts, we all hurt. When one person thrives, we all thrive. We should live with gratitude for the amazing gift of eternity given to us in Christ. We should celebrate life, abandoning our sorrows and receiving what was done for us years ago at the cross.

> *Every good and perfect gift is from above,*
> *coming down from the Father of the lights,*
> *with whom is not variableness, neither*
> *shadow of turning* (James 1:17).

The increasing rate of suicide is a disturbing phenomenon in our society. There is an incredible lack of patience and acceptance. Everything must happen as quickly as possible. Even dealing with a negative emotion is something we don't have tolerance for. We want immediate results.

I read an article about a military spouse who was dealing with her husband's depression due to PTSD. She talked about being patient and wanting to learn all about his mental disorder. She has love and tolerance for her husband in a beautiful way. She now helps other military families learn how to cope and live with PTSD.

I commend this amazing woman for her big heart and open-mindedness, enduring this test and becoming a witness for love.

Affection between couples is a completion of creation, a way for God to be glorified. It is not to bring us down to the point of death. If our feelings for a partner have any signs of codependence or neediness, we should step back and analyze ourselves, our partner, and our relationship with God.

> *Love is patient, love is kind. It does not envy,*
> *it does not boast, it is not proud. It does not*
> *dishonor others, it is not self-seeking, is not*

easily angered, it keeps not record of wrongs. Love does not delight in evil but rejoices with the truth. It always protects, always trusts, always hopes, always perseveres. Love never fails. (1 Cor. 13:4–8)

Humans often journey through life in search of someone or something that fills an emptiness in their lives. Even though we are not intended to be codependent on another person, we are indeed created to be together in pairs.

In Gen. 2:18, God says: *It is not good for man to be alone.* I have always wondered what Adam's behavior was before Eve was created, that had God thinking something was off. It seems that the Creator saw everything was good and He rested on the seventh day. The early stages of man's existence were clearly perfect and in good harmony, yet Adam's heart was not well balanced. It could have been that Adam saw all the animals in pairs and felt lonely, that he was not able to manage the garden all on his own, that he had to populate the earth, or all of the above. Regardless, there is a need we have for companionship that comes from the beginning of creation, and it sits deep within us. The Lord knew that giving man a perfect companion would be fulfilling for humankind and glorifying to Him. God created a seamless design to fill all voids and assist man in all areas, a being opposite of all man was but still equal. Someone to grow old with and share dominion over the earth, a helper to name all the animals, a hand to assist in the garden, and a wife to have children with.

However, God did not create another living soul so that man could feel that he was finally complete. Man was enjoying an amazing relationship with the Father, as we read in Genesis. The Lord walked in the garden with Adam. Man was already whole, with a purpose in his heart and a perfect fellowship with the Father. God's intention was for man and woman to share and complement each other, not to make each other whole.

Sadly, after the fall of man, this divine alignment was twisted by a force that causes oppression and control. Some men misuse their authority and instead of being protectors, they have become predators. Some women are no longer helpers but instead have become accusers and manipulators. Two of my girlfriends took their lives after engaging in fights with their significant others. And another friend ended his life after finding out his wife was cheating.

Society as we know it is twisted, making it difficult to live under God's given order. It is truly a fight few have chosen to fight. The original plan God had for mankind is not the chaos and desolation that we witness today. God's mercy is still for us and for those who have decided to take the steps to be aligned with the truth and endure until the end. Freedom and life in abundance are guaranteed. This does not mean we are exempt from hurt and disappointment. What it means is we find our strength in the joy of being in His presence and in the hope of His glory.

> *A cheerful heart is good medicine, but*
> *a crushed spirit dries up the bones*
> (Prov. 17:22).

We need to deliberately make a point to get to know who we are in the eternal kingdom and find purpose for our lives. Taking actions to fulfill goals and dreams, even the little things that make us happy, should be a priority. Reading the Word of God is essential because it is a powerful love letter from our Creator. It is the breathing Word and speaks to us in every situation. Meditating over this fascinating book will guide us to make wiser decisions. It will speak life and destiny for our path and for those around us. While we focus our mind on uplifting words, our breathing changes, and good things happen inside our body. The bottom line is when we starve ourselves of every good thing, we are giving way to anguish, torment, and death. God's communication to us was and is through broken people like you and me, who were selected to be witnesses of His love. The revelation we receive is a true testimony of freedom. It is bread to our spirit and soul. God's Word is living water to help in our lives.

REPLACING THE LIES

In the Bible, Satan is called the father of lies, as stated in John 8:44. Earlier in this book, I went over how the enemy will find any depraved circumstance in our lives to fill us with negative thoughts that are contrary to the knowledge of God. He is seeking to replace the spirit of truth with lies.

One of the first things the enemy uses against us is our physical appearance. Satan likes to pervert and twist all the beauty made by the hand of the greatest artist of the universe. He will constantly murmur in your ear that you are ugly, or overweight, or too skinny, or too short, or too tall, or not smart enough, or whatever else makes you believe you're not a magnificent piece of art, spoken into existence by our loving God. If we could only see ourselves the way He sees us, Satan would have no power.

There is a famous verse in the book of Jeremiah used to encourage people who are going through rough moments. It says the Lord has good plans for us, that He is not seeking to hurt us but to give us a future. Yet sometimes we believe the opposite. We lack confidence in ourselves and our abilities. All we hear in our mind is, "Your life is horrible. You have nothing but a past filled with bad experiences. You were rejected and offended; therefore, you are marked for a destiny of unhappiness."

Jesus told His loved ones in Matt. 28:20: *Behold, I am with you always, even to the end of the age.* But, how many times have we felt alone in the world? Abandonment is a common feeling in these times. We believe the lies that no one loves us, no one cares for us, and no one will ever help us. These deceits remain in us, and we accept them and become one with them. We try to cope and live with the false misconceptions of who we are made to be. The lies become our reality instead of living in the truth of how God loves us.

We must choose several times throughout the day to demolish every internal argument that sets itself up against who we are in Jesus. Taking a five-minute pause to breathe and fight for positive thinking is vital for our mental, emotional, and spiritual wellbeing. Sometimes we may need to take more than five minutes and be courageous in asking the Holy Spirit to reveal to us the negative or traumatic moments that need healing. There are some memories that could be buried deep inside our subconscious, either by our own choice or because we were too young to remember. God is in the deliverance business. He is pleased to set the captive free and heal the brokenhearted. According to His Word, if we ask anything in the name of His Son, Jesus, and if our request is aligned to His will for us, it will be granted to us. I believe with all my heart that there is nothing more that God desires but to see us free from transgression. Requesting from the Lord the revelation of past painful memories will allow us to realize the lie we accepted at the time. Then we get to renounce the lie and replace it with a true positive statement that is recorded in the Book of Truth.

When a person lives with constant negative thinking patterns from bad experiences, they will only manifest repeated harmful experiences. The hopelessness that comes with living a damaging life that repeats itself can open the door to depression, or worse, suicide.

We must accept only the truth and nothing but the truth. It is hard to discern what is legitimate when all we hear is deception. We should find courage in God, so that we can ride the wave without getting eaten by sharks. We should use all our inner strength to soar above the harmful thoughts we come across. There are multiple tools we can use and lots of resources out there. I will share some strategies in a later section that helped me stay in the path of clarity. The Bible is, without question a powerful weapon to help us win the battle. It is a book that speaks about being accepted and restored. We are loved beyond words, which is evident in the fact that Jesus died for us.

Jesus, the KING of the universe, died for you and for me. How much more can be done to show us the reality of who we truly are?

Living in the light of this pleasing revelation is not the same as shaking a magic wand to instantly turn things around. We can't expect to say a prayer and have our life change for good, forever. God is not our personal genie in a bottle. We must cooperate and act in ways to bring about our transformation. The Holy Spirt will fight for us, to help destroy the old patterns that are in us, even from our ancestors. We will start to use better judgment when it comes to the people we allow in our hearts. We will start to make better choices in every area of our lives. The Lord will come through for us, but we must be open to restoration. God does not need our help, but He wants us to invite Him to move on our behalf. As we yield to His Spirit, we will start experiencing a modification of character. At this point we should be proactive about making tangible alterations in the material world. We should let the flow of the newness manifest all around us—a new outer reality for the new inner us.

The old saying, "Rome was not built in one day," is accurate for any great empire. The kingdom of God is inside us and all around us. It will take a while to get to that perfect place, and it is probable that we will be working on it for the time we are on earth. The Bible says we are transformed from glory to glory. That means a little at a time, but never backward and always forward. There is another promise in scripture that says God has started a good work in us (through the spirit of truth), and it will not stop until the day of Jesus' return.

Cheer up! Deny the lies, receive the truth, work hard, be patient, remain strong, and test what grace and love are capable of.

WE ALL WANT TO BE ACKNOWLEDGED

Since infancy, all humans desire recognition for our abilities, whether it's saying our first words or taking our first steps. People thrive when they hear words like *well done* or *good job*.

We like knowing what we do matters and that we are important and needed.

It's heartbreaking for a child who is on stage during a school performance and sees several parents in the audience but not his/her own parents. It can be so painful coming home from a long day of work to an ungrateful spouse or disrespectful children. It is miserable to promise our lives to someone who does not want us or does not appreciate our efforts.

The Word of God tells us that God knows everything we do. We are not saved by good deeds, yet we will be recognized for eternity, receiving crowns of Glory for our performance, as kingdom ambassadors. The scriptures contain many references of promises for everlasting joy, but they also refer to rejection. We can face persecution, if we decide to take our cross and follow Jesus. Jesus said that the world will hate us, because of Him, and that our good doing is not going to be received or even acknowledged. So, if God knew we would encounter feelings of disappointment and that people would reject us, He has strategies for victory.

The first thing we should realize is that there is no greater acknowledgment than being chosen to be part of the great kingdom of Yahweh.

Can you appreciate it is not by chance that you are reading this book? God knows you by name, and He recognizes every little thing you have done for others. However, the Lord does not want you to only do for others. He wants to be your first love as you are for Him. He wants a relationship with you, more than anything.

So why not show Him acknowledgment and love back? It takes two to tango, and it's no different when it comes to developing a connection with our Creator. Acknowledge Jesus as the Son of God and what he did on the cross for you. Acknowledge that you are loved beyond what you can even imagine. When you think no one notices you, He assures you He knows the number of hairs on your head. When you think you don't look good enough, He says you are wonderfully and fearfully made. When you think no one cares about you and that you are just a waste in this world, He thinks you are worth dying for.

We will not always be recognized for our good doings, and that can be hurtful. However, if we change our focus to please Him, we will obtain far more blessings. We will get the richness of His glory and the hope of His calling. Our lives will become purposeful and joyful. The cares of this world will not be as important, and the ways that people treat us won't affect us as much anymore.

TAKE CHARGE

Be sober, be vigilant; because your adversary
the devil, as a roaring lion, walketh about,
seeking whom he may devour (1 Peter 5:8).

We are called to be sober and vigilant; this could refer to having a sound mind and not letting harmful thoughts enter in. It's important to recognize the dominion we have been given over our feelings. If we have control over our appetite when we are hungry, or over our bladder when it's time to go, or to avoid falling asleep when is not appropriate, that means we are in charge! We are capable to dominate our bodies and our mind. We can regulate and decide what thoughts we are going to accept. It's time to stop dark thoughts from ruling our lives. We can regain authority by consciously thinking what we choose to think. The Bible tell us in Cor. 10:5 to take captive every thought and make it obedient to Christ.

We must also be diligent in listening to our bodies and recognizing what medicines agree with us, either natural or pharmaceutical. If we require medicine to help us stabilize our moods until our emotions are handled, then we must be wise and do what is right. The Holy Spirit guides us in every area of our lives. We get to choose whether to take substances that alter our minds. Some can be helpful, and others can hinder our progress and throw us into a deeper mental melt-down. Medicine or any substance we ingest can be a means of coping with our problems. It's best to use them as a crutch until we learn how to give our problems completely to God. For some people, recovery can come right away, while for others it comes later. And, for some it can be a thorn in the side, as Paul has written about in 2 Corinthians. God is here for us, to love us, and to restore us. I believe that if we do our due diligence and get in tune with our minds and bodies, we will find the wisdom to discern what thoughts to let in. We can decide what people to let in our circle. We can choose what substances and food can lift us up or bring us down. We can also select what inner voice we choose to hear.

RELATE. WE ARE NOT ALONE!

This space is dedicated to you and me and to everyone who has a story, a broken heart, a crushed sprit, and the endurance to hold on, knowing there is hope.

The people interviewed on the following pages have gone through depression. They disclose their experiences with the hope of helping others. Some of these people decided to disclose their names, while others preferred to be anonymous.

Anonymous
Have you experienced depression?

Yes, I think so. I was never diagnosed, because I didn't go to a doctor to be treated, but I'm sure I dealt, and still deal, with depression.

What would you describe as the symptoms of depression? How did depression make you feel?

It made me feel hopeless and weighed very heavily on me. It's hard to "do life," hard to get ahead. When I'm feeling depressed, I sleep a lot more than my regular hours. I just go to work and come home to sleep. There's no motivation for anything else.

Have you always dealt with depression?

I can't say that I always had it, but it feels as if most of my life I have been dealing with it.

How old were you when you had your first depression "attack"?

I was eight years old.

Did something happen in your life that marked you deeply? And, if so, do you think this triggers your depression?

I was four or five years old when my stepfather molested me. He would come into my room and get in my bed. He touched me and did all kinds of sexual things to me. I thought it was an expression of love for me. I thought he was "loving me." I knew it was wrong, but at the same time it felt good and loving, so I never stopped him. I used to feel very shameful. On one occasion, when he was very new in our lives, he

French kissed me, in front of my mom, in the car. I felt very weird about the whole situation. My mom came into my room that night to talk to me. She excused him and told me he was just being funny and playful and he "licked" my face to play with me. One day at school we had some type of educational orientation with some bears teaching us about "good hugs" and "bad hugs." There was a girl in my class that was ugly to me. She told about an experience she had with a "bad hug" and that made me afraid to tell my story, because I did not want to become ugly too.

I had a lot of feelings of shame, self-hatred, and anger toward my mom, rebellion. I was violent.

My stepfather's sexual abuse stopped as I grew older; however, by age eleven I was having sex with my seventeen-year-old stepbrother. It gave me a sense of security. For some reason, I've always seen sex as something that makes people feel better. At least that's what I thought I was doing for my stepfather, and it helped me to deal with the guilt.

Have you contemplated suicide?
When I was a little girl, maybe around eight or nine years old, I just wanted to end the pain. The shame and guilt were too heavy to handle.

The thought of hurting my Nana prevented me from doing it. I also believed that suicide was the only sin you couldn't repent, and that scared me too.

Based on what you're telling me, would you say depression is a lack of something in your brain or a foreign, negative entity bullying you with what hurts you the most?

I never went to the doctor, because I didn't want them to diagnose me with some physical condition. I was afraid of being labeled a person with mental issues, so instead I used to cope with drugs. I had to do drugs to bring me up to speed and make me feel like I didn't care about anything. Depression does feel like some weird wall or heaviness that's hard to explain. I do believe it is spiritual too. I feel like I fight something that clogs my judgment and tells me that I'm not good enough or I'm a failure.

When depression attacks, do you know how to fight back?

I pray a lot when I start feeling it coming down on me. I make a list of negative thoughts and scratch them off to release them. I also make lists of positive things to remind myself. I'm certain that words have power. I really don't like pills, so when I'm feeling weak, I prefer to reach out to people and vent. I don't want to go back to my old ways and use drugs to calm me down.

Justin

Have you experienced depression? What are the symptoms?

Yes, I've dealt with depression on and off for a long time. I'm not sure about the symptoms anymore. It's hard to tell nowadays. I've learned a lot of coping mechanisms. If anything, I would describe it as boredom mixed with sadness. When I get depressed, it seems that I'm not even able to do the little things I could do normally, like hiking or playing video games. I'm not able to find something to entertain myself. It's maybe just a perspective of how I saw things when I felt depressed. The only thing I was able to do was eat, so I gorged until I gained over seventy-five pounds. The doctors diagnosed it as a chemical imbalance, and they prescribed antidepressants. I was on medicine for a while. They put me on lithium, but it was only to mask the pain. It was not a cure.

Have you always dealt with depression, and are you still affected by it?

If you've never experienced depression, it's hard to explain. It's almost like a demon that hangs around and sometimes you don't notice it and it doesn't bother you, but it's always there.

My mom was bipolar, and we grew up with her strange behavior. She didn't take medicine until the age of forty! We just learned how to manage. After my divorce, it felt like depression manifested more, because I was exposed to all kinds of changes, including the fact that we moved from Colorado to Phoenix.

What marked you deeply in a negative way in your life?

When I was a kid, around six years old, I was sexually abused by an older girl, who was a family member. I was a kid, so I wasn't able to recognize what was going on. It was not until the rejection happened a couple years later. I actually bonded with her in a weird way at such a young age. It was at her thirteenth birthday party when I was rejected by her, because she was older. I was eight years old then. I called her out when I was eighteen and she apologized; however, it didn't help, because she's a narcissist and it didn't feel genuine.

The divorce was very hurtful too. It made me feel worthless. It was very dark to my soul. I was battling depression while I was married, but my wife would use that against me. She didn't help me at all. She only made the feeling worse.

Have you contemplated suicide?

Enough that emotionally, I can still feel the pain. It's all rooted in feeling rejected and unloved. To me, suicide is a harder way out, because you know the impact the act is going to have. You know the sadness it will produce for everyone. Honestly, I think it's not about revenge, or attention, at least for me. It's just that you cannot handle the anguish. It was all about ending the discomfort, the pain of the heart. For me it was not a loss of hope, it was a desire to be done with the situation. I took antidepressants, because I totally thought it was my fault that my marriage was bad. My ex-wife suggested I take them, so I did. The antidepressants didn't help at all. I had the worst symptoms—sweaty hands, upset stomach, and insomnia, combined with a feeling of being a superman of some sort. It makes you feel super bad physically, and at the same time makes you not care about anything. That is one of the major reasons we divorced, because I didn't care anymore, at all, about anything. It makes you, mentally, feel amazing but in a weird, careless way. Antidepressants are the worst. I don't have anything in my brain that needs something like those pharmaceuticals. Our body is supposed to cure itself. If you find the code to unlock the cure to your body, you will be fine. Good food, exercise, meditation.

Based on what you have told me, would you say depression is a lack of something in your brain or a foreign, negative force bullying you with what hurts you the most?

I think it's all about perception or point of view. Perception of what was happening to me, to my ego. My view of things was not allowing me to see the big picture. You cannot see through the fog. The fog is literally like a curtain. It doesn't let you see what's happening around you. I think your experiences condition you to a feeling. When you ingrain it into a pattern, then your brain is conditioned, and when you are out of that pattern, your brain is out of whack. Some people embrace change. God gave me the ability to have a different perception of change. We know that as Christians, when we die, we go back to God, no different from any other culture or religion. The soul goes back to the source. We don't understand too much about God, who gives us this experience to make us human. I do believe Satan is the master of tricks; he has changed everything around to a devotion to himself. He has lied to us and made us think we do not need God and we have the choice to believe what we want. That is the separation, and Satan lies to me and makes me feel like I am separating from God. He makes me believe I am abandoned. Our main fear, as humans, is to be separate from God. Humans let humans down. The whole purpose in life is to understand that people will fail you. We must work at making relationships, even when we know people will fall short of expectations.

For me, spirits are outside entities or even, maybe, an alternate personality that we create. I don't think of a spirit as something going around telling me something. It's more or less to have some doors open. I don't know if spirits go around. Maybe they do go around, finding holes in your shield. It can also be that we allow them in, we invite them in.

It could be that the key to depression is to find that very thing in life that we respond to. Discovering that one thing in our journey that we are drawn to. Do not open the door to the physical vibration that is out there. Don't let in the shadows. Shame can be an open door, because it keeps you going back to that place of sorrow and reminds you of the separation. It's almost going back to the original sin. Close the door, go back to the garden, and go back to God. Spirituality is the main thing that helps depression. There is a Japanese scientist who teaches about how water freezes into different shapes, when he speaks positive words to it. When he speaks hateful things to it, the bubbles look different. The power of vibration literally infects the cells. The thing that travels faster than light is the spirit of love, the power of thought, the power of love. We have the power to curse and to release a curse.

When depression attacks, do you know how to fight back? What is your way to cope with it?

Gratitude pulls you out immediately. I make a mindful effort to be grateful. It is the main thing that helps depression. Earthly pleasures will do the opposite of what you are trying to fulfill. There is no amount of food, sex, or money that fills the void. The only way to find peace is to quiet everything. Sex fills a void temporarily. But, as soon as the action is over, the wounds remain, and they only get deeper. Cutting off a lot of toxic relationships also helped. Taking care of your body with nutritious foods and giving yourself positive fellowship. Paying attention to the people that really matter. Spending more time devoting myself to finding the spark inside me. Seeking the kingdom of God first. He calls all of us, but not all of us listen. When I listen, in my quiet time, I prosper. When I pay attention, it is amazing what happens. Lots of people are not listening because of shame or pain, but he is talking to all of us. Jesus was the first to teach us how to do it. He was here for us to follow Him; He was the Rabbi to teach love, to teach us to love ourselves. He allowed that connection of love to be apparent when He went to pray. He never prayed in public. He gave thanks in public, but He went away to pray. Time alone with God teaches us silence and solitude, it teaches us that the essence of God is inside us. If we open ourselves to that darkness, it will creep in. The most dangerous thing for humans is to be in a bubble and not allow the perceptions of others to guide us. We are supposed to be sociable, not isolated.

Pastor Eddie

Have you experienced depression? What are the symptoms? How does depression make you feel?

Yes, I have. I used to feel lethargy, inability to focus, confusion, and inattentiveness. My thoughts couldn't flow together. My pattern was all messed up. It could be just a specific thought or everything. At its most, it's an indescribable pain in your whole body. Like if you have kids and they want to go to the park, and you do not want to go. It has nothing to do with loving them, I just could not go out, did not want to go out. Every time I would go out, I had to put on a mask to be in front of people. I felt very broken. When you have that much despair, better known as clinical depression, nothing seems to work. The affliction I experienced could bring most people to their knees. Folks will want you to be sociable and enjoy being outside. Pulling yourself up, going out, and being around others does not fix it. Most people cannot handle you anyway, because you are so negative and a downer. So, you feel like you live in this isolated bubble of pain that you cannot get out of. The only way I can explain it is like having the flu. The only difference is with the flu you lie around for two weeks and it starts to get better. But with depression, after two weeks nothing changes, and then two weeks are four weeks, and then six months, and then it turns into years. People may understand pain, yet when the hurt lasts that long, it brings hopelessness. It is here when individuals start thinking, "Forget about it. It's better to die than to keep up with this pain."

Have you always dealt with depression? How old were you when you had your first depression attack?

No, I didn't always deal with depression. I was twenty-seven years old when I started to feel the first signs of depression. It was after a breakup that everything was triggered.

Did something happen in your life that marked you deeply? Do you think this triggers your depression?

When I was seven years old, my father announced to us that he and my mother had made the decision to divorce. I felt crushed thinking my father was never coming back. He also left the church. I felt rejected and abandoned.

Later, when I was in the eighth grade, I experienced verbal abuse from children at school. The mean things they said and all the names they called me only increased the feeling of rejection. That went on for several years. When I was finishing high school and into my years of college, I decided to leave everything behind. I started to dive into sexual sin and became a womanizer, hurting myself even more. This altered my personality. I was angry, bitter, and did not care about others. I was demonized.

At twenty-seven, after the end of my relationship and feeling the heaviness of depression, I finally gave my life to the Lord. I started to live a Godly life, yet I was still shattered inside. That is when the spiritual warfare took place. I started to experience the Holy Spirit and was filled up with inner healing.

Have you contemplated putting an end to your life?

I was never suicidal. I never wanted to end my life. I had a couple suicidal thoughts over the years, just short periods, and they were unwanted. They were not chosen; they were thoughts that were implanted there.

I believe depression is a very complex disease. I say disease, because your body is also affected. I am certain that medication works. You will be ready to take medication if there is no other resolve. I believe it can be a temporary solution to help balance you until you get other help. I have taken antidepressants, and they worked for me. They helped me to stabilize, but I feel like they masked the root cause. I wasn't able to feel how my soul was damaged and how it was messing up my body.

Depression is a deep pain. It's not like losing your dog. We just lost our dog, and we were very emotional about it for a few days, but it doesn't bring disruption to your life. Grieving is a normal part of life. Depression feels like death. When we talk about the realm of the corporeal, that's where doctors work. They deal mainly with the physical realm, which is the brain and chemicals. But now they're accepting that when they combine medicine with talk therapy, they are seeing good results. So, they are starting to step into the realm of the soul.

But we as Christians have the soul realm with the Word of God and the realm of the Holy Spirit reality in our spirit. And we have the reality that we fight against principalities and powers and demonic spirits. We see the whole picture. Most psychiatrists think we are crazy for believing in that realm. But that realm is real! A lot of what they are doing is only masking the depression. It may help people by making them feel better, but they are giving over to a lifetime of this, if all they do is take medicine. They may come out of it with counseling. But there is a whole realm in the spiritual that is understanding how to war in the spirit and how to live a healthy life. There are some people who go dark into the demonic realm. And it is all demonic to them. But they have not learned how to have proper boundaries. You must learn how to put limits on all your relationships. You do not want to allow people to control you or make you emotionally unstable. Even people within the church sometimes try to manipulate and control. When boundaries have been broken for so long, it is a process to deal with and to rebuild.

Based on what you have told me, do you think depression is a lack of something in your brain or can it possibly be a foreign entity bullying you with what hurts you the most?

I think it can be both. Demonic powers can affect the spirit, which also affects the body. The evil spirits are connected to those wounds. It becomes a melting pot. Demons plus wounds, they get to your mind through lies. They will whisper false realities about those experiences that marked you. It's like having another entity living inside.

When depression attacks, do you know how to fight back? What are your ways to cope with it?

Getting good sleep is really important for me. Making healthy choices for sure. Medicine is only a soul wheelchair; not making you walk is only holding you back. You do not want depression to become your identity. I get deliverance prayers over and over and seek inner healing. Now, I take a holistic approach to help me with the effects to my body. I pursue all the help in the way God open doors for it.

I had chronic depression for thirteen years of my life, but after faithful prayer and living for Jesus, I have been set free!

Mary

Have you experienced depression? What are the symptoms? How does depression make you feel?

Yes, I have dealt with depression several times in the past.

I used to feel extremely tired, sleepy all the time. All I wanted to do was sleep. I felt very lonely, but not in the usual way of feeling alone. It was an empty sensation I've never felt before. Sadness goes away; depression is a constant feeling of sorrow that lingers. It affects you emotionally and spiritually. You carry this emotion with you always.

How old were you when you had your first depression attack?

I was thirty-three years old, and I was already saved. When I came to the United States, it was a cultural shock. The different language, the culture. Coming to the States was a huge change that I was not prepared for. Only by the grace of God was I able to make it through. I really felt as if my life was falling apart.

Did something happen in your life that marked you deeply? And do you think this triggers your depression?

When I was five years old, one of my brothers molested me. Being sexually abused by anyone is horrible, but when it's someone in your own family, that makes it completely destructive. I understood it was not right, even when I didn't know about sexual sin, yet my brother was shady. He would tell me not to tell anyone about it, and because I was a child, I felt I was doing wrong. I started to feel anger toward my mom, because I felt she was not protecting me. That went on for some time. Then when I was thirteen years old, we joined a very legalistic church. We were not able to do a lot of things that are normal for most people. The pastor at that church presented me with fear. Even knowing they were abusive with the congregation, I started to experience calmness and somehow, healing started. He contributed a lot of knowledge about the Bible, which started to make sense on the way to deliverance. However, knowing all things about God, I was still feeling really hurt and felt bitterness toward the pastor and the church. But, not against God. I was mad that they did not help me. At the age of twenty is when I became really promiscuous. Lust became an addiction; it was instant gratification that I was using to cope with the pain.

Have you contemplated putting an end to your life by suicide?

Yes, I did think about finishing all the heartache that the transition to a new country was bringing me. I was desperate. If it had not been for my son, who I hold dear to my heart, I would have attempted suicide. The thought of him alone and dealing with that pain stopped me multiple times.

Based on what you have told me, do you think depression is a lack of something in your brain or can it possibly be a foreign entity bullying you with what hurts you the most?

I think it's a combination of both. If I'm not doing well spiritually, I can feel it in my body. When I start to experience aches, I know I'm not doing good in my spiritual life. There was a demonic intervention due to the lack of guidance. Since childhood, I had no direction, and even later, with the spiritual leadership I was exposed to. They did a good job helping me to believe that God exists. However, they did not help me with the feeling of loneliness and the belief that no one loves me. That is where the doors to depression open.

When depression attacks, do you know how to fight back? What are your ways to cope with it?

One of the first things is to repent. Repent for believing Satan's lies, but also for not believing and trusting God. When God says He loves you, it is because He does, and it's that simple. Also, I realized there were people in my life that really cared and were there for me. I started to acknowledge them and enjoy great fellowship. I started to open my eyes to positive things and not dwell in the negative. Before when I was depressed, the negative was overmagnified. When I decided to leave depression behind and experience freedom, a lot of the teachings I learned when I was younger started to make sense. I joined a great group called *Cleansing Streams* and that played a big part in my healing.

Alice

Have you experienced depression? What are the symptoms or how does depression make you feel?

Yes, I have experienced depression. I feel disconnected from people, and I suddenly start to become antisocial. It's a weird feeling where you are not able to feel any human connection. For some people, they experience weight loss and others experience weight gain. Some people do not go out of their houses at all. You get nervous when it comes to having a conversation with others.

I usually feel tired, sleepy, and isolated. At the same time, I experience insomnia, which is very bizarre, since you are always tired.

It's an inner pain that never goes away.

Have you always dealt with depression?

I was prescribed sleeping pills when I was five years old. I was having trouble going to sleep, because I had the impression that I was going to die in my sleep. I had the worst night terrors. My mother practiced Santeria, and it felt very heavy in her house. My dad, who is a Christian, used to pick me up to spend time with him, and that was the only place I was able to rest. I was not able to talk about the fact that my insomnia was directly linked to fear.

How old were you when you had your first depression attack?

My first depression attack happened when I was sixteen years old. I was a young girl, carrying a baby. I disconnected from everyone and hid my pregnancy for five months. Following that, I suffered with postpartum depression. I wanted nothing to do with my child, and it was a lot to handle for that age. I was really overwhelmed, and maybe I was a little selfish too. It was two months before I was able to take care of my girl.

Did something happen in your life that marked you deeply?

My mother gave me up to my dad when I was six months old, and I was reunited with her at the age of five. I lived with my mom until I was eleven years old. Living with her was torture, and I always had the feeling of death. I cried so much every time my dad dropped me off at her house, after spending the weekend with him.

When I was twenty years old, I was pretty reckless. Even when I was trying to be happy, I had a spirit of sadness. It was at this age when I had my first panic attack, and from that day forward, I have dealt with severe episodes of these attacks. I have pushed so many people away, because of this weird feeling. When I was thirty years old, we were with my family celebrating New Year's. I had a severe panic attack; they took me to the doctor and then I started with therapy. The therapist made me really mad, though. Some doctors seem as if they do not care about you. However, after taking a personality test that was more like a questionnaire, he told me I have an extreme mood disorder and that I was borderline bipolar. He prescribed me every type of antidepressant to help stabilize my moods. Some of this medicine does help, but you experience side effects, like insomnia and anxiety.

My mom was not very nice to me. I always felt very lonely, because of her. Everyone in my neighborhood did stuff with their moms, but not me. She was never home, and she never did anything for me. I do not remember her ever buying me anything. I felt like a walking zombie, so disconnected, and no one was able to understand me. At school I was a leader. I had a completely different personality than at home. I used to choose personalities to not let people at school see my sadness and anxiety.

Around seven to ten years old, I also experienced sexual abuse by one of my brother's best friends. I really did not know what was going on when this was happening, I was just scared. I'm not sure why I felt scared, but I had that horrible feeling inside. He used to come around and touch me in my private parts. When I realized what was taking place, I felt shame and even more abandonment. I told my mom about it, and she called me a liar. She did not believe me.

My kid's father hurt me very much, so he contributed greatly to my depression. He had me and my daughter, Sarah, in bad living conditions. We used to live in a motel, and I was very embarrassed with that situation and sad for my little girl. The way he used to hurt me paralyzed me. I could feel the pain deep in my heart and soul. Then the brain starts to play tricks on you. I started hearing very audible voices that told me no one loves me.

Have you contemplated putting an end to your life by suicide?

I have never contemplated suicide. Now that I'm older and can understand my condition, I have thought maybe if I were dead, all this would stop. When I get those thoughts, I start praying and thinking about God's goodness for me. I have realized I'm worth God's promise. I have never actually hurt myself...no. It has run through my mind, though.

Based on what you have told me, do you think depression is a lack of something in your brain or can it possibly be a foreign entity bullying you with what hurts you the most?

That is a tricky question. Mental illness is a big deal, and some of us need extra help. I think it is more chemical. It is an imbalanced chemical that does not allow us to process our emotions well. I do believe Satan takes advantage of the situation to fuel you with fear.

When depression attacks, do you know how to fight back? What are your ways to cope with it?

It takes me a couple days and sometimes even one week to realize when I am going through the depression cloud. I make myself leave the house, to maybe go shopping. I take it one day at a time. Sunglasses are huge for me, because when I wear them, it makes me feel invisible. It's funny but it's the smallest things that help. Since I am aware that it is a chemical imbalance, I am also looking into some natural ways to help my brain. I read the Bible to calm down. I am pro marijuana; it helps me, and I am able to relax and worship. I take less medicine if I do cannabis.

Scott

Have you experienced depression? What are the symptoms? How does depression make you feel?

Yes, I have experienced depression. It's a feeling of sadness, the extreme hopelessness you feel when it seems as if things will never get better. I felt like I deserved it. I gained weight, had lots of insomnia, and even had a heart attack.

Have you always dealt with depression?

Not always. I experienced anxiety as a child, but depression came to me later in life.

How old were you when you had your first depression attack?

I was thirty years old when I experienced my first episode of depression.

Growing up, I had a terrible fear that I cannot describe, and I never told anyone. I remember when I was in elementary school, my teacher brought some eighth graders to my class. The eight graders took us outside for recess. I don't know why, but I was terrified, shaking, and I didn't understand what was going on.

When I was five or six years old, I was separated from my family, and all I can think of is the fear that I felt from the separation that stayed with me.

When I was in my thirties, I started to get very sad and hopeless. It was not an emotional situation but more like something that came upon me all of a sudden. It was as if a cloud sat over me without warning. It was so heavy and dark. Very tangible.

I contemplated talking to Dr. Phil, so he could help me figure things out. I was pointing a lot of the blame on my wife.

Did something happen in your life that marked you deeply?

My best friend in high school was hit by a car, and I saw him lying on the ground. I drove by him, and he was lying in the street. There were people around, helping him. I felt guilty, because I was going to another high school. I was kicked out of the high school I went to with my friend. I would have been able to be with my friend if I hadn't been kicked out, so he wouldn't have been hit by the car. I suppressed feelings of shame.

Later in life, I lost my job on the police force. They brought someone else in to replace me, and that person only wanted to benefit himself. I started to feel guilt again and felt like I let God down. I always had the desire to help people, but I wasn't able to do my job anymore. I was experiencing PTSD from a lot of different events in my life. One traumatic event, while on the force, was witnessing an accident where the car had rolled over on the freeway. There was a kid trapped in the car. I couldn't get him out of the car and he died. I believe I saw the little kid, standing next to the truck, while I was trying to get him out. I can't explain it. The counselor told me I had PTSD and I needed to start taking medication.

Do you think this triggers your depression?
PTSD has a lot of symptoms, including anxiety, depression, and suicidal thoughts. The PTSD I deal with is due to a lot of emotional traumas that started years ago, including my high school friend's experience. I was dealing with a mental disorder I didn't know I had, and I started self-medicating.

Have you contemplated putting an end to your life by suicide?
Yes, I did contemplate ending my life. The way I retired from the police force was not the way I planned. I wanted to be respected and keep a good reputation. That brought me into a deeper sorrow, and my wife was not supportive. Our marriage was falling apart too. I felt abandoned, but I kept on living, hoping someone

would help. The abandonment was the last straw that triggered me to end my life. I had a plan how to do it, and I was not afraid to do it. I was clinging to God, but I could not feel Him. I had no guilt for the thoughts of taking my life. The day I was planning to do it, I kept thinking, "This is the last day for me on this planet." I felt so hopeless, and there was no safety net for me anymore. I thought about my daughters, but I was so disconnected from reality. It was so bizarre. I felt like I was watching a movie of my life. I was not in my own body and had lost sense of reality. When I woke up that morning, I thought, "Today is the day." I was just waiting for the time when I was planning to do it, but for whatever reason, God sustained me that day. When I was going to the counselor, I never shared with her my suicidal intentions. I kept it to myself. I had a friend who knew about it. No one else ever even noticed that I was always in survival mode. My friend knew about my suicidal thoughts, and she took me to the altar for prayer. The pastor spoke some words of encouragement to me, but that didn't bring healing for me. I was too far gone.

The following weekend I was planning to attempt suicide while on a camping trip. I felt a spiritual attack, and I didn't think I would be going home after the trip. At one point, I begged God to help me. I don't know how or why I didn't follow through with the plan that night, because I was very confident I would attempt suicide.

After I made it home, I fell to my knees and I told God that if I was going to stick around, then I am His. He started to do an incredible work in my heart. Still the darkness would cover me, and I was not able to sleep. My daughter reached out, and she started coming to stay the nights with me.

Based on what you have told me, do you think depression is a lack of something in your brain or can it possibly be a foreign entity bullying you with what hurts you the most?
I think it's a chemical issue, because narcotics do help. However, I also think there is a spiritual aspect too. I don't believe it was my own mind contemplating suicide, it was more like someone or something was telling me to do it.

When depression attacks, do you know how to fight back? What are your ways to cope with it?
Exercising helps a lot. When I work out, I feel much better. Doing any activity that gets me out of the house is always uplifting. I always remind myself who I am. I am a Child of God.

I have many scriptures that have become my anchors—John 1:12, Romans 8:16, Philippians 2:16, Psalms 139, and Psalms 13:1–2.

INTERVIEW CONCLUSIONS

B ased on these testimonies, we can appreciate that depression is possible to defeat. Everyone who kindly opened up to share their stories are heroes of their own movies. They all endured, fought, and believed the best, regardless of how dark and hopeless the situation was. The remedy is LOVE, and it is available to anyone at any time. Love is the engine that prompts us to seek help. Love is our friends who pray for us or the hands that provide help when times are hard. Love is the doctor with years of schooling, who gives us medicine that helps us through the illness. Love is the energy that helps us out of bed and off the couch, so we can go out and socialize with others. LOVE is God—it has always been and will always be!

As for those of us who have had loved ones that lost the fight, ending their lives to depression, we can come together. We can become the voices and cries for those who have passed on.

TIPS TO HELP BEAT DEPRESSION

Disclaimer: Always consult your doctor or psychiatrist before starting any treatment. I am not a licensed therapist, but I am a witness of many victories like the ones in this book, including my own battles. I am being obedient and following the direction of God. I am allowing His Spirit to lead. His Spirit and wisdom are the reasons I wrote this book.

David defeated Goliath with a slingshot and by trusting the Lord. This chapter provides tools that can be your slingshot, with God's help, to fight the giant of depression.

Don't give up!

SPIRITUALLY

Receive. The first step to connect with our spiritual side is to connect with God, asking Him to come into our heart. The bridge to our Creator is in the shape of a cross and was carried by His Son, Jesus.

Jesus is always waiting for us. He wants us to open the doors of our hearts and let Him in. It's no different from any other relationship. All we need to do is acknowledge Him, thank Him for dying for us, and start a daily dialogue with Him and the Father. Pursuing a relationship with Jesus has been, by far, the best decision I have ever made. If you don't know how to approach Him and you need help, send me a message on www.lovingfirst.com and I will be more than happy to pray with you.

Worship. Worship is an attitude of the heart. It can be a state of constant awe and reverence toward our Father. Worship is an expression that is often demonstrated by praising, with music and dancing. I recommend challenging yourself to hear only uplifting music that leads you into praise and worship. Christian music and the artists who write and perform it has come a long way over the years. There is amazing Christian music, as well as other genres that talk about God, love, and beauty.

Read. Science has shown that reading has some health benefits, including helping with depression, cutting stress, and many other benefits. It also improves memory and empathy, and research shows it makes us feel better and more positive too.

The Bible is not an ordinary book—it is the living Word of God, embodied in paper. In general, the Bible consists of the history of man, from beginning to end, and man's relationship with God. It can also speak to you intimately when you read it in your quiet place. It has stories of people like you and me, who trust God and how to overcome giants. It is the most wonderful story of love and redemption ever written. Reading the Bible will give you a different perspective of the outcome of your circumstances and will give you an eternal way of thinking. There are other books to read that have been inspired by goodness too. Self-help books and daily devotionals are a great way to read scripture, with little explanation.

Pray/Meditate. Praying is an intimate conversation with the Lord. It is a way of expressing freely all of our emotions. Praying is no different from talking to your dad, your best friend, your spouse, et cetera. There will be sometimes when you just want to talk to God about your life, world events, or simply thank Him for all he has done. There will be other times when you want to request things for yourself, someone else, or you may just want to sit in silence, soaking in His presence. Jesus gave us an idea of how to pray as recorded in the book of Matthew. *Our Father which art in heaven, Hallowed by thy name. Thy kingdom come, Thy will be done on earth, as it is in heaven. Give us this day our daily bread. And forgive us our debts, as we forgive our debtors. And lead us not into temptation but deliver us from evil: For thine is the kingdom, and the power, and the glory, forever. Amen* (Matt. 6:9–13).

Prayers of deliverance are very powerful. There are people in the body of Christ whose gifts are to help others by setting them free from demonic attacks. Jesus' public ministry was mainly teaching, healing, and deliverance. He gave all His disciples authority over demons. By calling out, "In the name of Jesus," we have also been given the same authority. However, there are those who are specifically called to cast out demons as their ministry. I had the opportunity to be in a prayer meeting with people whose call was to help others from evil oppression. Deliverance ministry is not a common gift, but that day I was set free from bitterness and anger that I held for years after my divorce. It was a great experience, and I recommend these types of breakthrough prayers to anyone suffering from depression.

Meditating is good to practice and take time for yourself to just sit and be quiet. Taking deep breaths, filling the lungs with air, and giving oxygen to the brain is a very relaxing technique. When you slow your breathing, it has been proven that it naturally creates calmness and tranquility. According to the American Institute of Stress, twenty to thirty minutes of deep breathing daily is effective in reducing both stress and anxiety (Kane, 2020). Meditating can stop negative thoughts and worries and help keep our attention on the voice of the Holy Spirit. We may not always be able to hear His voice, but we can feel a sense of peace and liberation when meditating.

Fellowship. Finding people who are like-minded is very important to feeling connected and to growing. Joining a church, a small group, or volunteering is healthy in many ways. There is power in numbers. When we get together with other believers, we become part of a family that has been given to us for eternity. Having a family of believers creates an amazing sense of belonging, unity, and love. We were created to be in community, and even more so with those who belong to the Body of Christ. We need to love ourselves in a self-centered way but, with the purpose of being confident when helping and loving others. *As a prisoner for the Lord, then, I urge you to live a life worthy of the calling you have received. Be completely humble and gentle; be patient, bearing with one another in love. Make every effort* to keep the unity of the Spirit through the bond of peace (Eph. 4:1–3).

Gratitude. Being thankful in every circumstance is not as easy as it sounds. Many of us walk around with an ungrateful heart from time to time. People often have something to complain about on a daily basis, and I can also be guilty of that. I used to say things like, "I hate washing the dishes," and even though it's still not my favorite chore, I've changed the way I feel about it. I remind myself of how thankful I am that I have dishes to wash from a meal that I was able to enjoy. Looking at every little thing with a grateful heart is a game-changer. You can start your morning by thanking God for another day of life, for your family, for your kids, for the love of your life, for your job. Then you can go into more detail with little things like warm water in the shower, your coffee, the sugar in your coffee, the table, the spoon, the eggs, et cetera. It sounds funny, but it's interesting how things change when we are grateful for everything, from the little things to the big ones. When we thank God for everyone we love, including those who challenge our faith, we love more deeply. When we appreciate the trials in our lives, we get through them easier. We need to understand that sorrow has a positive effect on our souls and helps us to grow closer to God. Gratitude truly opens the door to a multitude of blessings.

EMOTIONALLY

Choose the right people. This is easier said than done; however, it is a must! Toxic people can be like a poison that drains your energy and brings you down. If you are in an abusive relationship, seek support and leave that situation. Broken people often attract other broken and dysfunctional people. With time, when we become closer to our Lord, we will make healthier choices. As a result, we will start encountering more positive people. I do believe we are a magnet that attracts what we have inside. It's certain that "if you want to soar with the eagles, don't hang out with the crows." We need to be strong and separate ourselves from people who are not building us up in any way.

Talk to someone. Talking is liberating. Complaining all the time is not the same as being open with our feelings. When we are able to express our feelings and vent, we will feel emotionally lighter, and with help we may find some answers and solutions. In the book of James, Chapter 5, it says to confess our sins to one another and to pray for each other. Only in sharing our true feelings with others will we find deliverance, healing, and restoration. I think that good, sound therapy or counseling is a great way to vent and get a professional opinion and guidance. Setting a time to talk to a good fried, family member, or the church pastor is always a good idea too.

Feel your emotions and agree with them. This is a practice that has helped me to deal with moments of anxiety. We are not always in touch with our emotions, even when we think we are. When we have an angry burst, do we know the root feeling that made us explode in anger? For example, if you have been waiting at a restaurant table for a while before your friend or date gets there and you're feeling irritated and angry, you need to ask yourself the reason you feel that way. Are you feeling neglected or disrespected? Pretending it doesn't bother you or brushing it off is not the best way to handle it. Getting extremely mad, to the point of causing a scene and saying something hurtful, is not the right way either. It's best to express how you feel by saying something like, "I felt alone and somehow neglected or disrespected when I had to wait so long for you to get here." This helps us with our boundaries and can free us from hurt. Openly discussing, without an outburst, gives the other person the opportunity to understand us better. In the same way, we need to ask the Holy Spirit to give us the wisdom to understand our true feelings behind sadness, fear, anxiety, isolation, frustration, addiction, et cetera.

Writing your experiences, feelings, and thoughts. Therapists often recommend that we journal as part of treatment. "Journaling helps control your symptoms and improve your mood by helping you prioritize problems, fears, and concerns. It is good to track your symptoms, day-to-day, so that you can recognize triggers and learn ways to better control them." (University of Rochester Medical Center, 2020) Keeping a journal helps us to identify negative thoughts and find opportunities for positive self-talk. I'm not the best at following a daily journal, but I have done it when I needed to get my mind straight from depressive or oppressive thoughts. It's good to follow up daily or even hourly, if needed. It's amazing how helpful it is when you can identify patterns in writing that you've experienced. I will sometimes write down on a piece of paper all the things that have, or can, harm me. Depending on what you are dealing with, you can write things like negative thoughts, negative experiences, toxic people, words that have been spoken to you that have labeled you or that you feel have defined you. Once you have this list, you can go to a place that you find relaxing and pray about it, give it to God, and burn the paper. Let the heaviness go.

Clean up. Cleaning up your space is more than just hanging up your clothes, washing the dishes, or dusting. Getting rid of unwanted items or clutter has a healing effect on the soul. I had an amazing experience with this, while I was passing through a spiritual crisis. I came across some videos and books about the importance of tidying up. I decided to go room by room and find everything that did not make me happy. I got rid of clothes, pictures, decorations, memories, and other things. It was an amazing journey. While I did the cleaning, I had conversations with God about the areas of my life that I needed to clear. I was physically letting the old go and making room for the new. I believe that everything we do in the physical realm has a spiritual effect. Everything we do in the spiritual realm shows up in the material world. The results were amazing. The atmosphere changed, my space felt lighter, and I felt relief. I recommend to everyone to get rid of the old and open up room for the new!

Speak. Words are powerful. We can use our words to declare and to affirm. Our words can build up or they can destroy. *Death and life are in the power of the tongue, and those who love it will eat its fruit* (Prov. 18:21). Repeating positive affirmations about ourselves has an incredible outcome. If a thought is a seed, neuroscience has proven that if we repeat the same thought for twenty-one days, it opens the seed in the brain, and in ninety days it blossoms into a permanent thought or habit.

Making declarations of faith for our future about events we want to see happen is like what the Bible refers to as life or death. We can call out our life by speaking good things to come to us or by adding negativity to our fate.

I recommend reading *The Sermon on the Mount* by Emmet Fox. He describes to us, in detail, Jesus' teachings and how they positively affect our lives, if we follow them.

PHYSICAL

Nutrition. We all have heard information about what to eat and not to eat to have a healthy heart or a healthy weight. Less often we hear information about foods that can affect our brain function or state of mind. There are great ways to give proper nutrition to our brain that can help with mood disorders.

Sugar is truly a silent and slow killer. In addition to worsening your body's regulation of insulin, sugar also promotes inflammation and oxidative stress. Multiple studies have found a correlation between a diet high in refined sugars and impaired brain function and symptoms of mood disorders, such as depression (SelhubMD, 2020). A University of California study showed that a diet high in trans fatty acids was directly linked to increased aggression. It appears that trans fats interfere with the brain's ability to produce and use omega-3 fatty acids, which lowers aggression (Mind Body Seven, 2018).

Lots of us think we are doing a great favor to our bodies by not consuming sugar but instead using artificial sweeteners with no calories. Aspartame, for example, has been linked to behavioral and cognitive problems like irritable moods, anxiety, depression, and insomnia. Look at the ingredient labels of most diet foods or drinks. And try to stay away from ingredients like aspartame.

Alcohol is a depressant that affects the brain's natural levels of serotonin and dopamine, which are considered the happiness chemicals. So, even when you think it has a positive effect, because of the initial boost, the ingredients in alcohol are really affecting the chemicals in your brain in a bad way.

Many foods are beneficial for depression. Beta carotene, vitamin C, and vitamin E have been shown to help with symptoms of depression. Beta carotene can be found in many foods, including apricots, broccoli, cantaloupe, collard greens, spinach, and sweet potatoes. Foods rich in vitamin C include blueberries, grapefruit, kiwi, and oranges. Good sources of vitamin E are nuts, seeds, and wheat germ.

Smart carbohydrates are a good option because they have a calming effect. Whole grains are a good example of smart carbohydrates, whereas cookies provide simple carbohydrates. Protein-rich foods like tuna, turkey, and chicken may help with serotonin production. Vitamin B12 is super effective against depression. You can find this vitamin in fish and dairy products, or in supplement form. Go outside and get some sun to naturally increase vitamin D in your body. Foods low in selenium are linked to mood disorders. Selenium is found in seafood, some nuts, chicken, turkey, and other foods. Omega-3 fatty acids are essential for healthy brain activity. Recent studies found that societies that do not eat enough omega-3 have a higher rate of major depressive disorders. Good sources of omega-3s are fatty fish (salmon, sardines, anchovies, and tuna) flaxseeds, nuts (especially walnuts), and dark green leafy vegetables.

I realize we are living fast lifestyles and cooking fresh is not always an option. There are many nutritional supplements we can take to ensure we get the necessary vitamins and minerals.

Exercise. Research shows that exercise is also an effective treatment against depression. For some people, it works as well as antidepressants, although exercise alone isn't enough for someone with severe depression, according to Dr. Michael Craig Miller. High-intensity exercise releases the body's feel-good chemicals called endorphins, but the real value is in low-intensity exercise, sustained over time. That kind of activity spurs the release of proteins called neurotrophic (or growth) factors, which cause nerve cells to grow and make new connections and help relieve depression (Harvard Health Publishing Harvard Medical School, 2019).

Some of the symptoms of depression include feeling tired and having no desire to go out. To fight against this, make a goal of going for a five- to ten-minute walk every day and increase the length of your walk over time. Playing uplifting music and dancing for ten minutes is another helpful way to fight against depression. Make a conscious effort to exercise at least three to four times a week. If you feel ready, join a gym, start hiking, cycling, swimming, or find another physical activity you enjoy. Joining a competitive league is also recommended. Playing a sport not only gets you exercising but can also give you community.

Rest. Lots of people report sleeping issues as a symptom of their depression. For some people, depression causes them to sleep excessively. For others, depression causes insomnia.

Getting a good night's sleep should be an important part of your plan to manage depression. When you are well-rested, you will have more energy, a more upbeat view of life, and better focus (WebMD, 2019).

Our brain needs a consistent sleeping pattern. According to sleep experts, we need to make sure we get eight to ten hours of sleep per night. It's important to go to bed around the same time every night. Research has shown that consistency in the time we go to bed and the amount of sleep we get ensures the body releases hormones at the right times to make us feel sleepy or awake. An inconsistent sleep schedule throws off the body's clock (Graaf, 2017). There are some natural medicines that can help with the anxiety that sometimes comes up right before going to bed. Personally, magnesium helps me a lot when I am having anxiety. I also put on Bible audio or the Abide app, and that's the best insomnia medicine for me. Having a good night's sleep sets the mood for the next day, and it's the best way to let our bodies recover and heal.

Nature and Animals

Forests, oceans, waterfalls, and other similar environments are charged with negative ions. Negative ions are believed to have biochemical reactions that increase levels of serotonin, helping to rid us of depression and stress. We should make a point to go to these places often, whether on a weekend or for a vacation.

Animal therapy improves our mood by releasing endorphins when we interact with animals. Visiting or volunteering at animal shelters can give you the opportunity to be around the cute little creatures and show them love. You can also look up services on pet therapy or animal-assisted therapy for a personal treatment plan.

FINAL THOUGHTS

Everything in life has as much power as we give it. I know from experience that when your mind goes down the rabbit hole, only a miracle can save you. I have gone through a time where I almost lost my mind, and I can tell you the only thing that kept me afloat was acknowledging that God could get me out, and He did! His love for us can reach through the fog. All you have to do is picture Him offering His hand to pull you out. Make the effort and extend your hand back, hold on to Jesus, and He will give you peace beyond all understanding.

I pray that this book has helped you in some way. I also pray the Lord gives you the strength and wisdom to use some of these tips to continue on your own personal loving and positive journey with Christ. For prayer and encouragement, visit my website at www. lovingfirst.com.

REFERENCES

Depression after Traumatic Brain Injury. (2010). Retrieved from University of Washington: https://tbi.washington.edu/wp-content/uploads/TBI_depression2012.pdf

Graaf, M. D. (2017). *Why you MUST go to bed at the same time every night: People with a strict bedtime are more successful, study reveals.* Retrieved October 13, 2020, from Daily Mail: https://www.dailymail.co.uk/health/article-4597868/Why-bed-time-night.html

Harvard Health Publishing Harvard Medical School. (2019). *Exercise is an all-natural treatment to fight depression.* Retrieved October 13, 2020, from Harvard Health Publishing Harvard Medical School: https://www.health.harvard.edu/mind-and-mood/exercise-is-an-all-natural-treatment-to-fight-depression

Kane, S. (2020). *Why Deep Breathing Helps Calm Anxiety.* Retrieved October 13, 2020, from

PsychCentral: https://psychcentral.com/blog/why-deep-breathing-helps-calm-anxiety/

Mind Body Seven. (2018). *Anger Management: How Food Affects Your Mood*. Retrieved October 13, 2020, from Food and Mental Health: https://www.mindbody7.com/news/2017/12/18/anger-management-how-food-affects-your-mood

Selhub MD, E. (2020). *Nutritional psychiatry:Your brain on food*. Retrieved October 13, 2020, from Harvard Health Publishing Harvard Medical School: https://www.health.harvard.edu/blog/nutritional-psychiatry-you r-brain-on-food-201511168626

University of Rochester Medical Center. (2020). *Journaling for Mental Health*. Retrieved October 13, 2020, from Health Encylopedia: https://www.urmc.rochester.edu/encyclopedia/content.aspx?ContentID=4552&ContentTypeID=1

WebMD. (2019). *Sleeping Well at Night Can Ease Your Depression*. Retrieved October 13, 2020, from WebMD: https://www.webmd.com/depression/depression-good-sleep#2

WebMD. (2020). *What is Depression? | Understanding Sadness and Clinical Depression*. Retrieved October 13, 2020, from WebMD: https://www.webmd.com/depression/guide/what-is-depression#1